FIGHT
PEACE

DEVOTIONAL

FIGHTING WITH
PEACE

DEVOTIONAL

Carrie Pickett

Published in partnership between Andrew Wommack Ministries and Harrison House Publishers

Woodland Park, CO 80862 - Shippensburg, PA 17257

ISBN 13 TP: 978-1-5954-8530-4

ISBN 13 eBook: 978-1-6675-0280-9

For Worldwide Distribution, Printed in the U.S.A.

1 2 3 4 5 6 7 8 / 26 25 24 23 22

To my sister Julie and our family
who fought with peace and saw
the glory of God's love revealed!

Contents

Foreword

Fighting with peace, not a place of fighting against peace, but fighting *with* peace. You and the Prince of Peace, in partnership, operating with the confidence and boldness that together you have the victory. Not victory sometimes, or in the distant future, but a victory that you can declare to every part of your life in this world right now.

Peace is not a state of emotions, but it is a place of position. It's the Person of Peace that made a way of provision by His love so we now stand on the fulfilled promises of God.

Now with these promises, we war from a place of victory. The faith, courage, and boldness of God in us—His peace, His character of a finished victory. No fear, anxiousness, nor weapon formed against us can prosper. Because we not only fight with God's peace—it also guards our heart and mind in Christ Jesus.

In this devotional we're going to see who the Person of Peace is and how that Person of Peace now lives mightily within us.

If we don't realize our victory, we won't wield its authority and power. In these daily verses we're going to hide these treasures of finished work of Peace inside us so that today, no fear, no worry, no opinion of others can steal your God-given position of peace!

To winning each day,

Carrie G. Pickett

Let Me Show You, My God!

*And Gideon said to him, "Please, my lord, if the
LORD is with us, why then has all this happened to
us? And where are all his wonderful deeds that our
fathers recounted to us, saying, 'Did not the LORD
bring us up from Egypt?' But now the LORD has
forsaken us and given us into the hand of Midian."*

Judges 6: 13 ESV

I f there is one thing that disappointment and painful
events have taught us it is that they always offer the
opportunity to steal our peace. If we are honest,
we can probably say that we have expressed a little
of Gideon's attitude when we've encountered heart-
wrenching seasons or when things simply haven't gone
our way.

In these moments, it is almost always comforting to
get peace from an outside source. We call a friend; we

> ...if you know God as your peace...you will have courage to face situations and say, "Let me show you, my God!"

participate in someone else's self-calming exercise. We try a lot of different things to get to an emotional place of peace instead of looking within ourselves and declaring, *"Peace rules and reigns within me!"*

Ah, but here's the caveat: we must *allow* peace to rule and reign.

We serve a mighty God who is known by many names and by many attributes. We see Him as One who freely gives. He freely gave His Son that whosoever believes in Him shall not perish (John 3:16). This is not a command to believe but an offer to anyone who will *choose* to believe.

While this devotional is intended to show you how to stand from a position of peace, you must keep the Giver in mind. He *gave* us a free will and will never override how we choose to respond to Him or how we choose (or not choose) to respond to His Word.

In Judges 6:12, right before Gideon practically blamed God for his woes, God called Gideon a mighty man of valor. Here we see an example of how Gideon exercised his free will. Though God's word to Gideon should have been edifying and revelatory, it went in one ear and out the other.

The Lord then gave him instructions on how to save Israel, but Gideon was blinded to what he was seeing in the natural. He even went on highlight his inadequacies (verse 15).

Our enemy is constantly trying to steal from us and tries to lure us into walking in fear, doubt, and worry. This life offers plenty to be overwhelmed by, make no mistake. There are doctor reports, there are heavy family situations, there is unsettling on the world stage that threatens our livelihood. Look left and right and there is a bombardment of some sort telling us what we need to believe and follow.

But if you know God as your peace, as your Jehovah Shalom, you will have courage to face situations and say, *"Let me show you, my God!"*

Child of God—you mighty man or woman of valor—you don't have to live with even the tiniest bit of chaos going on around you. You don't need to don the boxing gloves and enter the boxing ring. Victory has already been declared!

So, allow me to show you, my God.

Lord, You are the God of peace, Jehovah Shalom. I want to fully be able to walk in every season, under all circumstances, and declare that You are my peace. My fight is taking a stand, resolving not to being moved by the enemy. I am choosing to have a hearing ear and teachable spirit on this journey.

The Lord calls *you* a mighty believer of valor. What does that mean to you? If you struggle to accept that title, look up valor and choose a synonym that the Holy Spirit draws you to. Write down what the He brings to your mind as you meditate on that word.

Let His presence overtake you at this moment. Allow Him to highlight hidden areas where peace needs to reign.

_____

_____

_____

_____

For further study:
Judg. 6:1-15

Ask the Father to show you a fresh aspect of His love for you today.

DAY 2

Peace is a Person

Then His disciples came to Him and awoke Him, saying, "Lord, save us! We are perishing!" But He said to them, "Why are you fearful, O you of little faith?" Then He arose and rebuked the winds and the sea, and there was a great calm.

Matthew 8:25-26 NKJV

My daughter's frantic voice over the phone told me that the devil was trying to steal her peace. Hearing her sobs of anxiousness told me he was trying to steal mine as well! Elliana, my beautiful 12-year-old, entered the new world of seventh grade. Need I say more?

"I'm going to be scared all day without you, Mom!"

This isn't my daughter's normal response when we are apart. She was fixing her gaze and responding to external situations that were unfamiliar to her. I had to remind her that while I wasn't there with her, her

Savior was. She later told me that that was the very thing that helped her through the day.

> There never has to be a settled feeling in our emotions before we speak the victory that is ours!

We all endure situations that are unfamiliar or that take us by surprise. *I don't know what is going to happen with my job...The doctor just said my symptoms are a sure sign of...*

Uncertainties can cause a shaking that try to get us to meditate on what we see. We may linger on all the potentialities. Before long, uncertainties become our fixation that infiltrate our emotions. Then our words follow and take over.

And our words are powerful (Proverbs 18:21)!

As we give a voice to our fears, our pains, our uncertainties, we are speaking the enemy's language. When you don't feel at peace, the enemy works it to his advantage. He acts quickly to make sure you continue to perceive things bigger than *his* enemy (God).

Take the example of the disciples in Matthew 8:24-26. They stayed fixated on the tempestuous weather and thought that they would die. All that panic while the Person of Peace lay sleeping nearby.

Peace is not an emotion. Peace is a Person. There never has to be a settled feeling in our emotions before we speak the victory that is ours! Rather, we need to remain confident in who God is and His promises about our situations.

When we get a revelation that Jesus lives inside us, we can speak peace over our emotions, over any situation! We should never let the enemy tell us what is wrong, how we feel, or how someone else's story will become our story.

So, when everything around us seems to be the cause of our condition, we look inside at the Person of Peace who lives in our hearts. We minimize problems by telling them how big our God is. We ask the Holy Spirit to bring truth and His promises to our remembrance.

My daughter's peace returned when she was reminded of truth.

God never develops a blind eye to our situations and then leaves it to us to figure things out. He calls us mighty men and women of valor for a reason: He is in us, He is with us, and He is for us. And if He is for us, no one dare be against us (Romans 8:31)!

Lord, You have made Your home with me, I never have to fear. I invite You into my situations and expect transformation. I endeavor to let peace be in charge over my emotions. I choose truth over what I see in the natural.

How do you perceive Proverbs 18:21? Can you identify any communication that has or has not been declaring life? What fruit have your words brought forth?

_____

_____

_____

_____

If you find situations and emotions veering out of control, read Romans 8:31-39 in the Message Translation. Make it your boast!

_____

_____

_____

_____

For further study:
Judg. 6:14-16.

Remember to ask the Lord to show you
how much He adores you today!

The Integrity of His Name

For to us a child is born, to us a son is given; and the government shall be upon his shoulder, and his name shall be called Wonderful Counselor, Mighty God, Everlasting Father, Prince of Peace.

Isaiah 9:6 ESV

If we are not careful, we can get too familiar with the names God identifies Himself as. And it is the enemy's greatest pleasure when we dismiss the incorruptibility, the impeccability, and the respectability His names convey.

We may not initially verbalize it outright, but our thoughts and our actions will eventually spill out into our communication. The world we are trying to reach with the Gospel hears one thing, but the turmoil we express outwardly communicates the opposite.

He is either our wonderful counselor with spot-on directions, guidance, and answers; or He isn't.

We either see Him as a mighty and all-powerful God who saves, rescues, and transforms; or we don't.

We can call Him an everlasting Father who cherishes, course corrects, and consistently loves us regardless of what we have ever said or done; or we can choose not to.

He has already delivered us from the tyrannical rule of darkness, settling His peace within us once and for all; or He hasn't.

I know that may sound intense, but so was the suffering of Jesus. His death fulfilled the Law and substantiated the fullness of His Person. This act alone forever gives integrity to His name, character, and nature.

God knows hell will be intense. He saved us so that we would communicate that the ruling and reigning work of the cross is the answer for all!

> God knows hell will be intense. He saved us so that we would communicate that the ruling and reigning work of the cross is the answer for all!

We want God to move and change our situations *yesterday.* Actually, He has. The work of the cross is finished, accomplished. When we choose to move toward Him when our hearts are hurried and worried, He will help us find a steady position of peace that can only be found in Him.

We've been witness to all kinds of global chaos. The world *throws up* its agendas and lies and lack of understanding. People are overcome with fear, angst, and even hopelessness.

All that is going on doesn't have to stress and mess with our peace. God is fully aware so we never have to pull a Gideon attitude that demands, *"Where are You, Lord?"* He has given us the answer: Jesus.

Reading the words, *It is finished,* means everything Jesus died for was accomplished. There is not another thing He needs to do. His finished work has provided!

When we are confident that His rule, His authority, and His peace dwells in us, we can *throw down* love, truth, and goodness back at the world. These are the declarations of a fighter who fights for the integrity of His name; a winner who knows who his God is.

Lord, thank You for all that You accomplished at the cross. My peace, my joy, my health, my prosperity, have been forever settled. Help me to lean on You and accept Your help when times get confusing; not only on a grand scale, but right here in my family, my job, my community. I want my life to declare the integrity of Your name.

Wonderful Counselor, Mighty God, Everlasting Father, Prince of Peace. This is just a short list of the names of God. What other names can you identify from the Word? Describe how they convey His character and nature. How has that name impacted your life?

Have you ever prayed for God to take all your problems away? Knowing that He has already finished the work to provide for everything, what steps can you take to fully comprehend the accomplished work of Christ?

For further study:
Jn. 19:28-30, Col. 1:13-14.

Lord, will You describe Your love for me today?

Peace is an Accomplishment

...and, having made peace through the blood of his cross, by him to reconcile all things unto himself; by him, I say, whether they be things in earth, or things in heaven.

Colossians 1:20 KJV

The enemy is ticked off! He sees the Holy Spirit's seal on believers and it reads: Taken!

The devil knows he cannot take us back under his rulership (Colossians 1:13). So, what does he do? He attempts to distract God's children with everyday issues that aim to steal our peace, kill our vision, and destroy our confidence in God (John 10:10).

When we are in the Word, we see our declared victory. But if we drift far from our meditation, the devil readily comes with his deception: *You've already spoken*

His Word; you haven't seen any changes. You should follow the doctors' advice, they're experts. Take a stand? You're just one measly voice.

His deception points to us, thereby drawing attention to ourselves. The more we look to ourselves, our flesh is quickened to seek answers on our own that we think will help rid us of the things that are stealing our peace.

Revving up our flesh is one of the devil's oldest tricks in the book. He diverts our eyes to worldly counterfeits that falsely promise a solution. Things that offer a *sense* of calm or make us *think* we'll feel better can take us in all sorts of directions.

Nothing outside of God's truth will ever offer sustaining peace. No pill. No attraction. No person.

Take time to read scriptures like Isaiah 41:10 that remind us that God is our help. Even though we have been freed from the dominion of sin, God understands that the devil looks for anyone who will give ear to his taunts and lies. Unfortunately, Christians are still targets.

> Peace is not a feeling; it is an accomplishment. Jesus made peace through His blood.

In late 2021, one of my sisters was diagnosed with Covid. Doctors' reports grew worse by the day. My family and friends immediately prayed and stood against this attack. We declared God's promises over her. We were a united front.

I remember, though, my heart and mind were attacked with thoughts of: *She could die! I'm going to need to help to be a second mom to my sister's children.* Other thoughts were invading and I felt like I had to truly fight to keep my peace and fight off feelings of anxiousness.

Yet, the Holy Spirit spoke so clearly saying, "*Get your eyes off of all that you see and don't focus on what you feel. Peace is not a feeling; it is an accomplishment.*"

Jesus made peace through His blood. He suffered intensely for reconciliation. We must not give place to taunts and misrepresentations. We need to tether ourselves to the truth of what has already been accomplished for us.

This was a heavy reminder that strengthened my resolve. I fought from my position of peace and victory by wholly considering His finished work!

This is the accomplishment that silences all counterfeit thoughts of unworthiness and inadequacies. He wanted all of us and saw us worthy enough to die for.

Jesus' sacrifice was no counterfeit. It was real and it's a done deal, sealed forever in the annals of heaven.

Attach yourself to that truth!

Lord, Your sacrifice satisfied everything! Help me to meditate on that daily. I trust You for wisdom in the things that are trying to take my eyes off of You and placing them onto myself. Thank You for comfort and encouragement.

Choosing to see that the blood of Jesus' sacrifice provides all we need is coming to a place of trust. We must decide to see that peace is ours in Christ regardless of what we see and experience. Ask God how He can help you consistently trust in His sacrifice.

Remember that our words have power for life or death. How can you partner with the Holy Spirit to help you guard your heart so that what flows from it will come from the Word?

_____

_____

_____

_____

For further study:
Col. 1:13-20, Jn. 10:10, Is. 41:10, Prov. 4:23

Lord, show me and teach me more
about the love You have towards me.

Believing Believers

For Christ himself has brought peace to us. He united Jews and Gentiles into one people when, in his own body on the cross, he broke down the wall of hostility that separated us.

Ephesians 2:14 NLT

Standing from a position of peace is an invaluable truth that bears repeating…daily. Our inheritance includes peace; so, meditating on and demonstrating peace is the impact we want to make. It is our legacy.

Inheritance is something given to us after someone dies. We receive a benefit that someone else worked for. When we talk about the finished work of Christ and how His sacrificial death provided all we need, the *all-we-need* stuff *is* our inheritance.

That may not seem like *new* news, but it seems that this news has been buried and forgotten. Evidence of strife and hostility is seen in the world, but we needn't look that far. One glimpse into our own lives reveal that we too have dismissed the inheritance that is ours. We see family disputes, church splits, denominational debates, even warring within our own minds.

The new covenant was birthed by Christ Himself at the cross, abolishing the Law that severely got distorted over time. The Law showed us that man needed a saving God. Instead, man worked the Law, trying to fulfill its requirements in his own effort.

Hostility was put to death and now Jew and Gentile have the same access to the Father (Ephesians 2:16); not through religion but through relationship. We all can be used by God, operating in that blood-bought peace, right?

That is only true when believers become *believing* believers—believers who understand that while we are in this world, we are not of it (John 17:14). We belong to another Kingdom (Colossians 1:13). We are Kingdom citizens with Kingdom rights. We are of a ruling class.

The devil doesn't want us to know that ruling and reigning runs through our veins. He wants our confidence in that finished work shaken. Any peace we do have is attacked on a personal level or by what is going on in the world: *"Hostility is everywhere,"* he taunts. *"Where is this peace God talks about?"* The devil awaits our agreement.

The truth remains: we have peace with God. There is no longer anything that separates us. We are free to come boldly and be in His presence; but we must *choose* to do so.

We can be told all day that we have received His favor, His grace. We have been justified,

and there is nothing we need to earn; but we must *choose* to believe that.

Believing believers know that God reveals precious keys to Kingdom living, keys to empowered living. Empowered living begins with love, but God doesn't stroke our feelings and say, *"Aww, did the big, mean devil attack you again?"*

No! He encourages us daily saying, *"Remember the cross and what it accomplished! Perceive this genuine love. You are victorious. I go before you in every attack. Understand you fight from a position of might and peace. Your pair of boxing gloves is my Word. Fight with My Word as your weapon!"*

The more believers believe, the sooner we will render the enemy's attacks as toothless acts of futility. We will then be used for God's purposes as ambassadors and invite others to partake of the inheritance. As freely as we have received, we freely give (Matthew 10:8).

This is legacy.

Lord, I am reminded that I am an ambassador of reconciliation. I belong to Your Kingdom. Everyone needs to know how much You love them. Help me to keep sharper focus on Your truths. As You have freely allowed me to come boldly towards You, help me to freely go and share Your love with others. I want others to join in this inheritance. I am choosing to be a part of that legacy by being a believing believer.

Free will is one of God's best gifts to us. Why is this so?

_____

_____

_____

_____

Believers believe. Are there challenges you face that make believing difficult? How can you solicit the Lord's help in these areas? Is He asking something specific of you?

_____

_____

_____

_____

For further study:
Eph. 2:14-18, Jn. 17:14, Matthew 10:8.

*As you go about your day, ask the Lord
to reveal more of His love for you.*

DAY 6

Reflect

F ighting with peace is posture, a position, a stance. The redemptive work of Jesus brought a peace between man and God. We are free to come into His presence free of guilt and shame.

I have illustrated the cover of this devotional journal with boxing gloves. Our fight is never a physical fight, but it is a spiritual battle. God is the King of the seen and unseen. He reigns; therefore, the fight is already won.

We fight to stand and to keep standing, using the weapon that is from everlasting to everlasting: His Word. When we as believers truly believe this, nothing that the devil or the world manufactures will last. His Word is the final authority.

Ponder on peace and how it was accomplished on the cross. Consider the full sacrifice. Peace carries the fullness of all who God is—His love, character, and nature. With all that has been discussed in days 1-5, do you find yourself positioned in peace?

Reveal

Attach yourself to what has been accomplished and given to you by Jesus' sacrificial death on the cross!

Telling people, *"Let me show you, my God,"* is never intended to be a delayed expression of praise that is only declared after you mature in the faith. Whether you are someone who has journeyed for awhile or new in your faith, it's about reflecting on the big and small wonders of God.

But I encourage you to say it anytime and anywhere. Whenever you experience the peace of God, shout it out, regardless of how long you have been walking with the Lord.

Speaking this aloud boasts of the faithfulness of God, thereby offering the opportunity to share Jesus to the world. Your words are seeds. One seed may land into the *soil* of a soul who needs to experience the peace you demonstrate.

Consider the following verses. Write anything that encourages you to shout His praises.

Phil 4:9 ESV: *What you have learned and received and heard and seen in me—practice these things, and the God of peace will be with you.*

_____

_____

_____

_____

_____

_____

_____

_____

_____

_____

_____

_____

Col. 3:15 TPT: *And let the peace of Christ rule in your hearts, to which indeed you were called in one body. And be thankful.*

Rom. 5:1 NLT: *Therefore, since we have been made right in God's sight by faith, we have peace with God because of what Jesus Christ our Lord has done for us.*

---

*When you keep your mind focused on
Him and what He has provided, you are
not just in peace, but perfect peace.*

Back to the Source

*I have told you all this so that **you may have peace** in me. Here on earth you will have many trials and sorrows. But take heart, because I have overcome the world.*

John 16:33 NLT (emphasis mine)

There is much to be said of having an intimate relationship with the Father, Holy Spirit, and Son. Each Person of the triune God offers His own individual characteristic in this intimate union. The Father provides a fatherly comfort and perspective. He is very interested in us—He created us (Isaiah 43:21)! He made us for Himself and He is the guardian of our souls.

The Holy Spirit is the revealer. He shares the mind of the Father and the words of Christ. Insight, wisdom, and truth are graciously unfolded; we just need to ask.

> Relationship is peace because we sit with the Person of Peace.

Straight from the heart of Jesus is where love is best demonstrated, mainly because we see Him in the Word as human like us. I may love my husband, children, and family, but Jesus loves them more than I do. He was the One who willfully laid His life down for all of us. His love is unparalleled.

If you'll recall, I found my heart wrestling to keep my heart in a place of peace when my sister was hospitalized with Covid. But like the caring Father God is, He took me aside into a one-on-one. The Holy Spirit gave me a Rhema Word, opening my eyes to see Jesus' sacrifice as an accomplishment. The Spirit told me that *in Him* (Jesus) is where I would find my steadfast peace and confidence because His sacrifice had already accomplished everything.

No other place offers a believer this kind of eye-opening revelation than in an intimate relationship. Relationship is peace because we sit with the Person of Peace. When we are *in Him,* we are in peace.

Jesus overcame the world. However, we still see signs of unrest, hostility. When we operate in love, peace, and truth, we will experience this kind of hostility because Satan sees our very existence as a threat. He knows we have the victory and tries to deceive us from understanding that.

Every hostile thing that *separated* us from Him was nailed straight to the cross: the grip of sin, tormenting shame, fear, self-condemnation.

Romans 5:1 offers a comforting truth. We have been justified by faith and, therefore, we have peace with God.

The more I have matured in my knowledge of Him, the more I find myself running back to relationship where my Source of Peace is waiting for me. What better place is there to go and get divine counseling and guidance and reminders of what is ours in Christ?

In this world we will have trouble, but in intimacy is where we stay in peace. There we find Grace extending it out to us every time. We just need to open our hearts and receive it.

Lord, I see that what You accomplished on the cross is foundational for my peace, my confidence, and my courage. Thank You that I am free to be in Your presence. Always guide my heart back toward intimacy and help me to open my heart for what You have for me there.

Jesus brought peace between you and God, no more barriers. Is there anything that you can identify that keeps you from coming *in full surrender* to Him?

Even with the surety of His peace, we will undoubtedly still experience trials and tribulation. Yet, His Word has the answers for all the *whys, hows,* and *whats* concerning some challenges you may be facing. Do you have questions? I believe He has answers for you today.

_____

_____

_____

_____

For further study:
Jn. 14:27, Jn. 16:16-33.

As you go about your day today, in all that is happening around you, ask Him, "Lord, show me how much you love me today."

Fear Fills in the Blanks

Love has been perfected among us in this: that we may have boldness in the day of judgement; because as He is, so are we in this world. There is no fear in love; but perfect love casts out fear, because fear involves torment. But he who fears has not been made perfect in love.

I John 4:17-18 NKJV

When this verse talks about fear being a result of one *not* being perfected in love, it is not saying that we must perform so that our love is perfect toward Him. It is speaking of a matured understanding of God's perfect love toward us. When this understanding becomes a part of our who we are, fear has a hard time hanging around.

Maturity comes through an intimate relationship with God. The Lord knows everything and wants to download wisdom for everything, including how to deal with fear. We can only mature and develop confidence when we spend time with Him—*in Him*—and allow Him to help us find answers in His Word.

> When it comes to fear, the lines between lies and imagination can become blurred.

A good indicator of our maturity level is how we respond to fear. Now let me be the first to say, the devil will come after a mature believer as quickly as he will a baby Christian. If there is *any* response to even a tiny sliver of the devil's lies, the devil insidiously works with the hope of breaking us down.

Fear can take on different names: anxiety, worry, stress. It may be easy to think that there are legitimate reasons to be overwhelmed. The devil has devised an evil plan, using people, governments, and disease that wreak havoc in our lives if we let it.

Before we allow the enemy to take out his paint brush and smear images on the canvas of our minds and emotions, we need to discern what is a lie and what is imagination. When it comes to fear, the lines between lies and imagination can become blurred.

Everything that comes from the devil is a lie. That much we are certain of. He was a liar at the beginning and will be a liar to the end. But the more we respond to deceptive stimuli, the devil works on our imaginations.

Imagination and lies begin to blur when we give time to that first deceptive thought. *What if my boss makes a demand on me, I will have to... What if the economy keeps taking a dive, I just might... What if there is another pandemic, I need to make plans... The doctor says this is terminal, so, I must...* Fear has entered imagination and starts to fill in all the blanks.

The negative power of imagination is that we hear all the *what if* scenarios in *our* voice. We personalize the situation by putting ourselves in a possible future reality. We then share our concerns with family and friends. The devil sees that we took the bait and continues to paint even more futuristic pictures for us to meditate on.

A fear-induced future reality is where the devil wants your imagination to live. There is no peace in that, only torment.

This is why the Lord invites us all into an intimate relationship with Him. In John 16:33, Jesus told His disciples that *in Him* they might have perfect peace. This is for us as well. This position produces a baseline for a positive imagination where we paint an image of

God—His plans, His peace, His love—in our future. Relationship promotes healthy imagination to thrive.

God's love for us includes purpose for our lives, and His purposes are good. Relationship helps us see His Word come alive, birthed from the imagination His love perfects.

Lord, I want to mature in my understanding of Your love for me. I do not be want to be swayed by lies that want to overtake my meditation. Thank You for daily invitations to be with You. I am so awed at how You love me. Help me to clearly see when lines between lies and imagination are blurred.

There is no *fake it 'til you make it* with God. We can only declare the truth that we know. This is a result of an ever-growing and maturing knowledge of His love for us. If you find yourself wavering in His love for you, search the Word that speak of His love. Make these your meditation.

The opposite of fear is love. Explain this based on I John 4:17-18.

_____

_____

_____

_____

For further study:
Jn. 16:33, Jer. 29:11.

*Be sure to ask the Lord to show
you His love for you today!*

Speak Ill or Speak Will

Now faith is *the substance of things hoped for, the evidence of things not seen.*

Hebrews 11:1 NKJV (emphasis mine)

Back when I was in Bible College, Andrew Wommack was teaching his students to pray without ceasing. I remember thinking that was impossible. Not only did I have my studies, I had a job.

Andrew then turned the question around: *"How many of you can worry without ceasing?"*

To my 19-year-old mind, worrying was easy, hands down. But I clearly understood the point Andrew was making.

Similarly, Jesus gives us a point to consider in John 14:27b. He commands us to not let our hearts be troubled or afraid. If we are commanded not to, then it is very possible that we can *let* our hearts be troubled.

A lot of our heart trouble stems from the fear we allow in our lives. It is then reinforced by the words we speak regarding it.

A small rudder on a huge ship in the hands of a skilled captain sets a course in the face of the strongest winds. A word out of [our] mouth[s] may seem of no account, but it can accomplish nearly anything—or destroy it.

(James 3:4-5 MSG, brackets mine)

This is such a powerful verse! It tells us how important our words are. We must rightly choose what comes out of mouths—death or life (Proverbs 18:21).

Our tiny tongues are like the rudder of a ship and we are likened to the skilled captain who didn't watch his words. What our mouths speak affects our minds, our actions, and our peace. We set the course when storms come. We may not consider our words as *death;* but anything that doesn't speak life is death. Words of death attract Satan. He roams like a lion seeking whom he can devour (I Peter 5:8).

> Words of death attract Satan. He roams like a lion seeking whom he can devour.

Now, we have established that the devil can present distractions all he wants. However, he cannot drag Christians back under his rule. His distractions can pack a damaging and hindering punch to our assignments, and especially to our peace if we *let* them.

Look at Hebrews 11:1 again. *Now faith is*…faith brings futuristic hope and peace into our realities. Fear works the same way. Fear is always attached to the future: there isn't the evidence of all the unknowns, yet we let imagination explode with possible outcomes.

The moment we see anything that resembles what we have played out in our minds, we have the potential to turn fear into blame: *Where were You, Lord? You could've prevented this!*

What are our words going to line up with? Where are we going to let our rudders steer our ships? The world's opinions? The news? The declared Word of God?

Develop your skills to speak life—our voice is to sound like the Word! His will is laid out for us in His Word and we discover it in relationship. Let's speak His will, let's pray without ceasing, and park our meditation on His truths. Let's multiply our realities with hope and peace by tethering ourselves to God's will.

Now fear is…a liar! When we know this, faith is stirred and we can speak to our storms with authority!

Lord, I endeavor to not let my imagination be used for anything but hope. My hope is in You. You are my God and You care for me. I declare to see You in my future regardless of what I see. Your love never fails.

What declarations have been stirred up in your heart right now? Let the rudder in your mouth steer your heart towards Him and the goodness that He has brought to your mind.

Now faith is the substance of things hoped for, the evidence of things not seen. What do you not see? What promise from His Word can you attach your faith to? How will you keep that promise in front of you?

_____

_____

_____

_____

For further study:
Heb. 11:1-3, Jn. 14:27, I Thess. 5:17.

*As you go about your day, ask the Lord
to show you how much He loves you.*

God is a Show-Off

Rejoice in the Lord always; again I will say, rejoice.

Philippians 4:4 ESV

I was a little hesitant to title this *God is a Show-Off.* I didn't want to come off as irreverent or anything. After some thought, I decided that this is how succinctly I can explain how I see God.

God is in the business of doing immeasurably, abundantly more than we can ask, think or imagine (Ephesians 3:20).

Anytime we see God working on behalf of His children, there is grace—reigning supreme and raining down in exponential and unfathomable ways.

This is how to fight with peace. We declare who our God is! I don't think we can over exaggerate God and His goodness. Although, it sometimes appears that we tend to under exaggerate His omnipotence.

> Peace is in its truest manifestation when things are falling apart but we choose to stand regardless.

You might be thinking, *Yeah, but you just don't know what is going on in my life.* No, I do not. But even when the world is seemingly coming apart at the seams, God is always good.

The Apostle Paul sent his letter to the church in Philippi while he was imprisoned in Rome. He knew of the persecution that they were enduring but encouraged them not to be troubled, and urged them take all their concerns to the Lord. He also told them to rejoice.

Not just sometimes, but to rejoice *always.*

Undoubtably their trials were many. Why rejoice when resistance and persecution were at the forefront of daily living? Let's recap our *how-we-fight-with-peace* weapons:

1. We know that peace is not an emotion or feeling. There is no counterfeit comfort (no pill, no attraction, no person).

2. Peace is the fullness of God: the triune God dwelling within us.

3. Peace is an accomplishment. He made peace with us through His blood.

4. Peace is found in relationship.

These are some loaded weapons! Paul understood these truths and knew that peace would abound even in the midst of trials. Peace is in its truest manifestation when things are falling apart, but we choose to stand regardless.

This is telling the devil and the world, *No!* We will not choose your false way of peace. We choose to rejoice. It is difficult to rejoice with thankfulness and still be perturbed.

Not responding like the world will likely invite the gamut: others' opinions, personal jabs at our faith, a possible snickering rant against our God. They see the circumstances coming against us, but we choose to exhibit His peace.

Again, this is where the power of our words comes into play. We don't join in on conversations that speak death and hopelessness. We speak the victory that has already been declared. We speak life with authority.

This revelation raises an expectation that our God will show-off with immeasurably more than we can think and shower us with His grace over every area of our lives!

This is how we fight with peace. This is our witness. This is why we rejoice…always.

Lord, fill me to overflowing. I endeavor to be a witness to Your goodness, Your grace, Your love. I choose to rise above the confusion and half-truths that want to overtake me to opt for the world's peace. I choose You.

You may feel you have lost your witness and your first love. Will you be willing to trace your steps back to when faith and rejoicing was vibrant? I believe God wants to show you some things.

You may have not ever been taught all that was given to you when you received your salvation. Have you received any new revelations from what has been presented?

_____

_____

_____

_____

For further study:
Phil. 4:1-13, Eph. 3:20, I Thess. 5:16-18.

*Remember to ask God to show
you His love for you today.*

DAY 12

Offense/Defense

...do not be anxious about anything, but in everything by prayer and supplication with thanksgiving let your requests be made known to God. And the peace of God, which surpasses all understanding, will guard your hearts and minds in Christ Jesus.

Philippians 4:6-7 ESV

Just when you get to the point where you are feeling confident in your position of peace, the devil drops a little anxiety bomb.

This was evident when I was in Russia working to help lead and direct the newly established Charis Bible College. I was young, and much of my personal expenses were supplemented from state-side donations.

One particular occasion, this support seemed to be at a standstill. And, of course, everything that needed to be paid was due the next day. I could feel the anxiety rise.

I did what I knew to do: pray, confess that God was my source, rejoice. That would work for a minute; then fret, worry, and doubt

> There is only one Savior; and Savior is not our title.

came the next minute. This constant back and forth was debilitating and I got upset with myself. *Why, Lord, can't I be consistent?*

My frustration led me to confront my anxiety. After apologizing to God, He told me that every time I chose to turn from the flesh and turn to Him, that was a victory. *But I've wavered like one thousand times, Lord.* He assured me that I had one thousand victories.

That changed my perspective, and I saw an offensive and defensive inner working of faith.

We endeavor to stay filled with the Spirit as an *offensive*, preemptive measure to kindle our faith. God acts as our *defensive* guard offering peace when we come in gratitude and praise. He even offers peace when our offensive measures go amiss. What a trusted Savior!

When ministering peace to others, we too point them to the Savior. We can and should offer people comfort and our prayers; but part of ministering is sharing our faith and conveying the goodness of God. We show them His truth and promises in the Bible.

Sometimes though, we may encounter someone that depends on us and our faith. This has the potential for us to lean on our own fleshly wisdom to help them through a painful situation. It might be as innocuous as providing a service, maybe some money. But the flesh profits nothing, only the Spirit gives life (John 6:63). They need the Savior.

There is only one Savior; and Savior is not our title. We need the Holy Spirit's wisdom anytime we minister to hurting people who have opened their hearts to the lies and half-truths of the enemy. This is very difficult when this *someone* is a relative, or our child.

The problem with pain is that it hurts. So, as the Spirit leads, we remind them of who they are, whose DNA that carry (Galatians 5:22-23). We prophesy over them assuring them that there can only be a break-through, a victory. Peace is for them now and in their future because God is for them *now* and *in* their future.

You and I can say all the right things as we minister, but someone may reject our words. At the end of day, it will be the peace of God they will need to experience for themselves. We cannot allow anyone's rejection to steal our peace.

We all have the same choice. Free will is always involved. We pray that the people we minister to will see that they are playing *offense* on this spiritual battlefield. They already have peace; they already have the victory. We then trust God will provide the *defense*.

Lord, help me to point everyone back to You. As I minister to those You bring across my path, I pray for patience and Your wisdom. I want to be tender and truthful. Show me how to be a good steward of Your excellence.

Ministering healing and freedom and peace can be difficult, even when we are ministering to ourselves. What specific guidance have you received from the Holy Spirit for others? For yourself?

People can come to a place of desperation, and sensing their dependence on us can bring a certain threat to our peace. If you have been in this kind of situation, how did you handle it? Could it have been handled differently?

For further study: Jn. 6:63, Gal. 5:22-23 TPT.

Remember, the Lord is waiting to show you His love for you. Just ask!

Reflect

God is our source for peace. When we come to trust that, we will find it nearly impossible to look anywhere else: in the world, in ourselves, in our relationships. We can find some temporary peaceful things in all of those things, but lasting peace comes from God alone.

Free will is always involved in our decision making. We may not make all the right decisions, or choose the exact course of action, but God will not beat us up. He is the guardian of our souls. He is ever ready to come to fill and lead us with peace when we consistently come to Him.

We can minimize poor choices by remaining in Him, in our relationship. He will remind us how He has come through for us in the past, and tell us how He will be there for us in our future. He desires to show Himself strong on our behalf—the consummate *Show-off*.

Ponder all the ways the Father has come through for you, how His love and peace have been the foundation of your life and ministry. Remember we are all ministers. With all that has been shared on days 8-12, how have you ministered peace? How have you pointed others to the Source?

_____

_____

_____

_____

_____

_____

_____

_____

_____

_____

_____

_____

_____

His gives strength and might to His people
as they allow Him to be their Source.

Reveal

Speaking His truth is not only vital to stir our faith, but it is imperative to show the world Jesus. Philippians 4:5 reminds us to let our reasonableness be known to everyone. We are carriers of His DNA; we are to exhibit the fruit of the Spirit.

As fruit is demonstrated, we allow others to see Jesus. Let's act as the overcomers we are. Let us not hang our heads in defeat and succumb to what is thrown at us. Let us rise.

Rising is revealed most prominently in our speech, but it also is showcased in how we don't let another's communication corrupt our hearts. We are not moved; we stay in peace.

We can speak ill, or we can speak will. His will. Meditate on the following verses and write how they encourage you to live and demonstrate His peace to the world.

Jas. 1:19-20 ESV: *Know this, my beloved brothers: let every person be quick to hear, slow to speak, slow to anger; for the anger of man does not produce the righteousness of God.*

_____

_____

_____

_____

_____

_____

Prov. 12:25 NLT: *Worry weighs a person down; an encouraging word cheers a person up.*

_____

_____

_____

_____

_____

_____

Col. 3:16 GNT: *Christ's message in all its richness must live in your hearts. Teach and instruct one another with all wisdom. Sing psalms, hymns, and sacred songs; sing to God with thanksgiving in your hearts.*

When you speak peace over your storm with your authority, the storm hears His voice.

Perfect Peace

*You will keep in perfect peace whose mind is stayed
on you, because he trusts in you.*

Isaiah 26:3 ESV

One of my most heartfelt passions is to help people find their relationship *with* and *in* God. My desire is to se e people participate in this consistent, intimate relationship where they develop an unshakeable understanding that God is one hundred percent on their side.

I believe that this intimate union should be the believer's starting point in their day—it's their mind's inclination to be in His presence. Every waking moment is bathed in the knowledge that they are loved. Nothing can erase this *knowing* from their heart.

Perfect peace is attained when our minds are stayed on Him (Isaiah 26:3).

Am I perfect in doing what I teach people? No. I get invited, though, to be in His presence just like everyone else. And as I lean on Him, He gives me counsel and direction for the day.

> If God didn't expect us to live and be a conquering example by exercising our authority, He wouldn't have given us back the authority that Adam lost in the garden.

I have said it before, but I will say it again. Our peace will be found in relationship. There are too many things that vie for our attention and affections outside of this union. We've got the devil ready to aggressively deceive us, and the world (man) rousing us to follow his way.

We have already concluded that our fight is not an actual fight—the devil is a defeated foe! Jesus abolished the dominion of darkness on the cross. So, as we consider the cross, we begin to comprehend that our inheritance also came by His blood.

Sometimes we tend to forget our inheritance because we live in our earthly vessels and live in this fallen world. When we get the understanding that we have been translated into the Kingdom of His dear Son (Colossians 1:13) we gain a different mentality.

We have become citizens of heaven. Heaven is here and now. We are seated in heavenly places with Jesus (Ephesians 2:6). Our inheritance is in the spiritual realm, but we can experience its Kingdom benefits and power now.

We best express our inheritance when we speak with our authority against deception, sickness, weakness; against poverty, against depression. It's against the law of the Kingdom

for these things to *think* that they can attach themselves to us.

Herein lies the Advocate for our authority, the Holy Spirit. When Jesus left this earth, He gave us the most precious gift of the Holy Spirit. We have full access to this divine teacher, counselor, comforter. He goes with us wherever we are and in whatever situation we find ourselves in.

This relationship with the Holy Spirit helps us to keep our minds stayed on the Lord. He partners with us to lead and remind us of the truth when situations try to lead us down paths of deception and anxiousness.

If God didn't expect us to live and be a conquering example by exercising our authority, He wouldn't have given us back the authority that Adam lost in the garden.

With all this favor that was purchased by our Lord Jesus Christ, how can we not keep our minds on Him, being fully persuaded of His love for us? His blood, our inheritance, and our authority, becomes our stance to remain and to fight with the Prince of Peace, Immanuel, God with us!

Lord, I am beginning to understand how peace gives me confidence in how I fight. I need to have a working knowledge of that all that You have done was because of Your great love for me. Guide me today, teach me to always be ready to execute authority!

If you have never asked to receive the baptism of the Holy Spirit with the evidence of speaking in tongues, simply ask now.

What ways can you still your wandering mind and stay focused on Him? Peace is there!

_____

_____

_____

_____

For further study:
Col. 1:13, Eph. 1:18-19, Eph. 2:6, I Cor. 14:2, 4.

As you go about your day, remind the Lord
to show you how much He loves you.

Peculiar People

...no weapon that is fashioned against you shall succeed, and you shall refute every tongue that rises against you in judgement. The is the heritage of the servants of the LORD and their vindication from me, declares the LORD.

Isaiah 54:17 ESV

Fear is tangible. We can feel fear; and if we allow it to remain, we have all but given the devil a glorious victory. But we are certainly not those who are held back by fear and perish; we are among those who have faith and experience true life (Hebrews 10:39 TPT)!

This is what is meant in I Peter 2:9 KJV which states that we are a *peculiar* people. We define peculiar as odd or weird. Others might see us odd by believing and speaking the way we do.

> **Facts are temporal. Truth is eternal.**

However, another definition carries the idea of *belonging exclusively to; particular and special.* This defines God's children exactly. We belong to Him, we are particular, special, and stand apart from the world.

So, when fear attacks, we have to remember that we are this peculiar group who isn't held back by fear. This is how we combat fear. We immediately reject it so that it doesn't linger and infiltrate our thoughts, or sway us to respond in the flesh.

While there are tangible evidences that bring on fear, these are just facts. Facts are temporal. Truth is eternal. We have the authority to take fact into the realm of the supernatural. What is ours (inheritance) in the supernatural utterly consumes fact, reversing it, and completely taking it out of the picture.

The problem is that many of us have done that, but our situations haven't changed. This is why this series is called Fighting with Peace. When we have hidden His Word in our hearts, and understand Kingdom principles, we will see the devil for who he is. We fight to understand that he is *not* the final authority.

Our fight is to remain standing in peace no matter what the devil throws at us. He is like a lion, roaring divorce, sickness, impatience. He uses our personal pronouns when he lies. *I feel like... My back pain is... I am a failure; I can't do anything right...Could this be a sign that I am headed for...* We hear our voice speak the lie.

The devil doesn't stop at our own voice. He will use the voice of others. When we share our issues, people can chime in agreement, share their own experience, or even bring our past mistakes into the mix.

The truth that we know is what sets us free. When fear attacks, our response has to be: *Fear, you are liar!* We are the only ones who can give the devil permission to invade our thoughts. We can receive his taunts and lies, or we can rise up and say, *"Devil, who do you think you are?"*

We have the Holy Spirit, our biggest encourager, on stand-by all the time. All we need to do is ask Him for help. We can be perplexed about somethings that are causing tensions and fear, but the Lord knows everything and He will deliver us (Psalm 34:4)!

We need to utilize all that is in our peace-wielding arsenal: the Word, His Holy Spirit, our authoritative voice. Our pastor, our Bible study teacher cannot fight for us. They can agree with the Word with us, but we have the ultimate responsibility of how we stand.

We are peculiar people! We need to know who we are and to Whom we belong. We are God's chosen to be used for His possession. We have a role in the Kingdom and we masterfully execute that role from a position of peace.

Lord, I do not want to go from crisis to crisis, but from peace to steadfast peace. Thank You, Holy Spirit, for being my go-to whenever I feel anxious. I endeavor to seek You at all times. Help me use my available weapons!

Keeping the Word hidden in your heart is one of the best tactics you can use as a believer. Have there been things that have hindered your time in the Word? How can this be remedied?

The truth that you know is what sets you free. What does that mean to you?

_____

_____

_____

_____

For further study:
I Pet. 2:9, Ps. 34:4, Jer. 33:3, Jn. 8:32.

*Today, ask the Holy Spirit to show you
another aspect of His love for you.*

Vive la Résistance

Submit yourselves therefore to God. Resist the devil, and he will flee from you. Draw near to God, and he will draw near to you.

James 4:7-8a ESV

My husband and I used to own property that had a stream that ran across it. The current was pretty swift so my kids were very careful not to let any toy land in it. If one landed and the toy wasn't retrieved in time, it was gone forever, carried down and away off the property.

One day, my son Michael was feeling a sore throat coming on. We immediately prayed and spoke against it. He declared, *"Sore throat, you need to leave and fall into the stream!"* The stream became the family's proverbial dump site for lies the devil threw our way.

After praying, my son said he felt fine and went to play. Later, he complained that he felt the sore throat again. He then asked why it came back. He had a picture in his head that when he cast that sore throat in the stream, it would be gone forever.

> We have the power to tire the devil out with our bulldog resistance and tenacity, not the other way around.

The devil was painting a picture in my son's mind that God's Word couldn't be trusted; he was attempting to weaken my son's faith.

When it comes to fighting with peace, resisting the devil is something we do repeatedly. We have to speak against emotions and disappointments that may result from something that we thought was *taken care of.* We have to keep our minds stayed on the Lord for clarity.

I told my son that we are to be persistent in resisting the devil. We cannot let our guard down regardless of what we see.

If I can be honest, sometimes disappointment can stir up a lazy spirit. We may have stood against something, and even had others agreeing with us, only to experience disappointment later. Disappointment can wear on our souls and make it seem like we are in a losing battle. This is exactly where the devil wants us to land.

The enemy is relentless. He will try to attack over and over again whenever an opportunity arises. He has had plenty of time to master his plans of attack. He has been watching man's behavior and knows how things irritate us. How? We have given him a front row seat to our negative emotions, our faithless words, and our actions or inactions.

We cannot be passive but persistent in our resistance. John 4:8 tells us to draw near to God and He will draw near to us. When He's near, we can know His voice and follow His lead.

The key to this verse is that in drawing near to God we are reminded of our victory, our position, our authority. Resisting the devil is easy because we know that he no longer has any ability.

Vive la résistance is a *never-give-up* war cry. We have the power to tire the devil out with our bulldog resistance and tenacity, not the other way around.

Lord, help me to remember that the devil has no authority or ability to overtake my thoughts unless I allow it. I want to have a bulldog tenacity to resist. Help me to guard my heart and mouth so I do not give the enemy an edge with negative words or in how I respond to situations. Help me to submit myself to You; surrendering completely so that You can touch every part of my life.

What key actions are you employing to resist the enemy?

_____

_____

_____

_____

We never want to confess that we have had a lazy attitude when it comes to fear and disappointment. We cannot afford to be passive. What postures are you maintaining?

_____

_____

_____

_____

For further study:
Is. 35:4, Ps. 27:1.

As you go about your day, ask the Lord to
remind you how much He loves you!

Our Pursuit

I will listen [with expectancy] to what God the LORD will say, for He will speak peace to His people, to His saints (those who are in right standing with Him)—but let them not turn again to [self-confident] folly.

Psalm 85:8 AMPC

How badly do you want it?

This question tends to be delivered with an encouraging spirit behind it. What initially comes to mind is a football coach pumping up his team in the locker room at half-time.

But saint, how badly do you want the reigning and ruling peace of God in your life?

First of all, we believers have peace dwelling inside of us already. We have established that Peace is a Person. But, does *He* reign and rule?

> The main key to keep in mind is that in order to flee something, we need to be pursuing something else.

We might have a careless approach to manifesting this peace for many reasons. We say we want peace to be at the heart of every decision, but there are just other things more pressing at the moment. *Besides, peace isn't a real issue in my life. I make do; I maintain.*

We talked about having a lazy attitude when it came to resisting the devil; but that same attitude can be applied toward manifesting peace.

Run from anything that stimulates youthful lusts. Instead, pursue righteous living, faithfulness, love, and peace. Enjoy the companionship of those who call on the Lord with pure hearts.

(II Timothy 2:22 NLT).

This verse had been served up in every youth event that I can remember. However, youthful lusts and passions are not exclusively for the young. All this verse is conveying is that we should shun anything that persuades us to let it occupy the center of our world.

We want what we want, when we want it, and whatever it takes to get it. The world offers its own passions and will tell you that it should be yours. The world will also tell you how to satisfy each: education, family, love; what you need to be watching, where to invest, etc.

So, I pose the question again, how badly do you want it?

When we spend time in intimacy with the Lord, He will open our eyes to what is good and perfect for *our* life. All the stuff the world offers might not be necessarily bad, but God created you, died for you. You are a peculiar person, God's possession (I Peter 2:9).

Psalm 85:8 says that we should have an expectant heart. God loves us deeply; and when that truth is established within us, we are more apt to tune Him in to learn of His very best.

I like how Psalm 85:8 reads in the AMPC. It tells us not to return to *self-confident* folly. Other translations just read *folly.* Self-confidence can be a form a pride. We can trust in our education, our social status, our riches. Folly refers to lacking reverence and faith in God.

There is only one who knows everything and we need to be learning of Him, trusting His grace for everything. The main key to keep in mind is that in order to *flee* something, we need to be *pursuing* something else. Pursue the Person of Peace.

Lord, I sit at Your feet with an expectant heart. I am trusting You to give me a right-now word that will squelch anxiety and worry. Your counsel is the only counsel. Reveal anything that distracts me from my purpose and peace.

It is easy to convince ourselves that what might be satisfying the flesh isn't really causing harm to anyone. Take inventory of your pursuits and discuss things with your true counselor.

Can you see any pursuits that cry *Me, Me, Me?* God is a jealous God; His love burns for His peculiar people. He knows the very best for you. There is a grace to let things go. Let Him show you how.

_____

_____

_____

_____

For further study:
II Tim. 2:22, I Pet. 2:9, Ps. 85:8-13.

Ask the Lord to show you how much He loves you today!

Lovers of the Word

Great peace have those who love your law; nothing can make them stumble.

Psalm 119:165 ESV

Now that is a great promise! Having peace—great peace—would mean never having to have an internal fight over things like anger, offense, impatience. It would also include never having to stumble with wavering faith, unbelief; or having a see-saw relationship with the Word.

Those who love God and love His Word are blessed with this great peace. Peace speaks of direction. Peace keeps us steadfast: we will follow truth, we will trust in the unseen; we won't follow facts or emotions, or what is seen in the natural.

Peace also makes it easier to place people in the Father's hands—loved ones who have gone astray. Sometimes we feel it is our responsibility to point people in the right direction. When we entrust them to the Father, we know that He can touch their hearts better than we can.

> Great peace comes with a great fight.

Looking at the world around us, we see that standards are being lowered, constantly going down. We see it in our nation's ballots, the products we buy, in the service industry. Misled people only aim for excellence when it serves them best.

When God calls something great, it is beyond our imagination. Imagine God having a dictionary and we look up the word great? We would be blown away. So, when we allow ourselves to have relationship with the Word—loving it and pursuing it as our vital need—we receive this great peace.

Being fully persuaded of His love should drive us all to the Word because He always has more for us. He will reveal Himself and allow us to find and experience the riches of His glory. He says, *"I have this for you: My peace that will direct you to My ways and My thoughts. My Word is the standard. Following the standard upholds you."*

We all have to come to a point where we are tired of being tolerant; tired of being unfulfilled with the standard of the world. Our motivation should be for the truth that saturates every inch of our being.

Keeping His Word in front of us becomes a lifestyle. Our minds gradually transform as they become renewed to God's way, to His perspective, to His standard.

If you see yourself as one who vacillates between positive and negative responses to situations, may I remind you that God is for you. You are one of His chosen, He is not displeased with you; and you are never cast off because you think your life has been up and down. God's acceptance has never been about you, but what Christ did *for* you.

The world will speak its lies declaring how the Bible is irrelevant and outdated. They maintain their position because godly principles go against fleshly mindsets— mindsets that have been perpetuated and believed as the normal human response to life's issues. Many of the world's standards regarding life, regarding pleasure, regarding convenience, regarding justice go against the truth of God's Word.

Make no mistake, God will not be mocked. When we stand for God's truth, great peace is ours. Great peace comes with a great fight. Our hearts and prayers are for a misled world; but the world will ultimately answer to God.

Lord, I am grateful that I can lay every weight aside and fully embrace the truth that You are for me, You are my rear guard. Holy Spirit, teach me more about how peace will direct me; that it will help me know God's standard. Help me to not deviate from it!

Can you spend a moment and openly discuss your relationship with the Word *to* God?

If God were to have a dictionary that showed the definition of *great*, how do you think He would define it in regards to *great peace*? And what would His definition of great peace look like in your life?

_____

_____

_____

_____

For further study:
Rom.12:2, Jas.4:2-3, I Jn. 4:4, Ps. 34:14, Heb.12:1.

Remember to ask the Lord to show you
how much He loves you today.

Reflect

The Lord calls us His own. We are His peculiar people, chosen and forever cherished. Since we are His, He always has our best interest in mind. He is never out to shame us for not meeting His standard. He draws us in love to find *the* better way. His standard is the better way, His standard is His Word; His standard is peace. His way is stumble-free.

When we live from a position of peace, it acts as a directional sign post to stay on course. As the things of the world and the lies of the enemy relentlessly shout that there is another way, peace keeps us on the narrow path. This is not the path of least resistance, but a path of much resistance.

We are told to flee from youthful passions. The best way to flee something is to pursue something else. That something else is the Word. The Word will never steer us wrong!

Ponder all the ways God has demonstrated to you that you belong to Him. Is there any doubt that He is for you? With all that has been shared on days 15-19, can we agree that great peace comes with a great fight? It's a fight to resist, a fight to pursue and remain in His Word.

Setting your mind on the flesh is death, but setting your mind on the Spirit is life and peace.

Reveal

When we stand for truth, God stands with us. He becomes our rear guard. He protects our hearts and encourages our spirit. We are never left unprotected.

Standing and resisting lies is strengthened by how fervently we pursue His Word. His Word guides us into all truth. We all need His guidance and direction. When things seem too hard, He invites us to press in all the more.

We've all heard seasoned believers say that they are *still* learning, *still* growing. But even what "little" truth we know is powerful. Declare what you know. Let what you know transform your hunger for more.

Meditate on the following verses. There is peace in knowledge.

Prov. 15:16 TPT: *It is much better to live simply, surrounded in holy awe and worship of God, than to have great wealth with a home full of trouble.*

Col. 2:8 TPT: *Beware that no one distracts you or intimidates you in their attempt to lead you away from Christ's fullness by pretending to be full of wisdom when they're filled with endless arguments of human logic. For they operate with humanistic and clouded judgments based on the mindset of this world system, and not the anointed truths of the Anointed One.*

Jn. 17:3 ESV: *And this is eternal life, that they know you, the only true God, and Jesus Christ whom you have sent.*

_____

_____

_____

_____

May grace and peace be multiplied to you in the knowledge of God and of Jesus our Lord.

Lions and Bears

Moreover David said, "The LORD, who delivered me from the paw of the lion and from the paw of the bear, He will deliver me from the hand of this Philistine."

I Samuel 17:37 NKJV

The story of David and Goliath depicts how good triumphs over evil no matter how big the problem. A youth with his sling, one momentous event; that is all it took.

David was ready for this confrontation with Goliath because he had already experienced prior victories in the fields as a shepherd. David was entrusted to watch over his father's flocks. That meant he cared for their needs and for their protection.

His heart was for the sheep; so, when a lion and a bear attempted to *steal* for a meal, David killed them. That was no small feat, but God was with David. God had plans for David.

I had to bring this story to my daughter's remembrance. I had shared earlier how Elliana experienced some anxiety and fear upon entering seventh grade. She had overcome much of the trepidation, but later she began experiencing physical ailments.

"These are weapons of the enemy," I told Ellie. "When the devil can't break you with one weapon, he will try another, then another. He tried fear and anxiety; he painted pictures of some things that caused you to worry. You overcame them; but now he's trying the weapon of sickness. The devil doesn't let up, he is after your peace and confidence.

"But this is where you stand and resist again, just like David," I continued. "He wasn't going to let the *weapon* of a lion or the *weapon* of a bear steal from the flocks. The fear you felt, that stomachache that wants to keep you from school, those represent a lion and a bear. They want to take you out; so, you need to resist and tell the devil, "*Not on my watch!*"

This is the attitude we all need to maintain. The devil will harass and employ any weapon to see if we will get

> Who is this uncircumcised Philistine, that he should defy the armies of the living God?

weary and stop resisting. The devil's agenda is to steal, kill, and destroy, but Jesus came to give us life with abundance. This is why we must hide the Word in our hearts.

In this world we will have trouble (John 16:33). But the hidden Word is to be unsheathed and used as our weapon to combat the devil's lions and bears. David saw Goliath as another beast. David's resolve rose up and he believed that God would deliver him again. His attitude revealed his confidence: *Who is this uncircumcised Philistine, that he should defy the armies of the living God?*

We all have had unwanted and unexpected lions and bears that made a horrible noise! David used his past victories to solidify the truth of His God for future victories. *He will deliver me from the hand of this Philistine.*

This is where we apply Isaiah 54:17. No weapon formed against us shall prosper, neither shall the accusations or judgments the devil wants to tear us down with. We have a better weapon, the living God and His living Word inside of us, the Prince of Peace. We will shut the devil's mouth and tactics. Authority is our heritage. God Spoke it.

God not only spoke it, but He demonstrated it on the cross. It's good overcoming evil, no matter how big the problem.

Jesus, the Good Shepherd, was entrusted to care and protect His Father's flock. He knew the lions and the bears would attack to devour the sheep; but He took care of their every need and their protection by giving up His life for them. This sealed everything.

This Man with His cross, one momentous, veil-ripping event; that is all it took.

Lord, thank You for reminders in the Bible—Your truths for victorious living. I refuse to live paralyzed by fear, but choose to paralyze fear with fearlessness. I praise You for what You've accomplished for me.

What lion or bear is presently making noise? What Word can you unsheathe to silence your enemy?

Recall a past victory. How did the event prepare you what you may be experiencing today?

_____

_____

_____

_____

For further study:
I Sam. 17:4-37, Jn. 16:33, Is. 54:17.

*Be sure to ask the Lord to show
you how much He loves you.*

DAY 23

Headless Giants

Today the LORD will conquer you, and I will kill you and cut off your head. And then I will give the dead bodies of your men to the birds and wild animals, and the whole world will know that there is a God in Israel!

I Samuel 17:46 NLT

David spoke some powerful fighting words to Goliath. One just doesn't throw words out like this in the heat of a challenge. There has to be some faith behind them. David's words were not a mere threat; he knew his God, he knew the strength of His God, and he trusted in the delivering power of his God.

So, after Goliath's taunts, David used his sling, brought Goliath down, and followed through with his promise. He went to his enemy, used Goliath's own weapon, and cut his head off. He finished the job.

Sound familiar? *It is finished!*

Can we make a similar declaration like David to our situations? Are we ready to cut off any giant's head?

There can be no wavering behind the authority that was given to us. Our peace is an accomplishment, meaning we can *rest and trust* in the authority that is ours. We either have faith in that accomplishment or "hope" that our words will work. The latter isn't an option.

We must understand that even though we have a physical body and live in this physical world, we are not of this world, nor do we wage war as man does (II Corinthians 10:3). Our battle is against spiritual forces in heavenly places (Ephesians 6:12). Our faith in the resurrection power places us in right-standing, which gives us a powerful inheritance.

And a big part of that inheritance is that we can operate with the same authority Jesus did here on earth. We don't have to wage war in our strength and knowledge, function our lives based on man's standards. When the world is running from counselor to counselor, from doctor to doctor, from marriage to marriage, we can dig our heels in and say *No!*

The war against good and evil is a story that earthly history hasn't closed the book on; but in the spiritual realm, yes! It's a done deal via the blood of Christ! When Jesus breathed his last, the Law, fear, sickness; all the lies of the enemy, and sting of death were destroyed once and for all.

Jesus went to hell to take the keys from the enemy. It was like David's final blow to Goliath. Something without a head is nothing. Jesus rendered the devil headless.

Peer into the spiritual realm and see that the enemy has no authority. He cannot unless we follow our flesh and allow him into our situations.

Declare with me that we will choose our Father, we will choose to follow after peace, we will not shrink back in fear. This doesn't mean that this is the end to distractions, taunts, or even to questions that rise up on our end.

Instead, we will choose our blood-bought authority and walk in it, and continue to walk in it. Every noisy lie that wants to invade, we will declare like David, *"Today, I will cut off your head!"*

Lord, You told Your disciples that they were going to go out with signs following, performing good deeds and that nothing deadly would harm them. I take that directive and go in Your strength and might with the authority You have graced me with. I know that if things get heavy, You will be helping me along the way.

Be mindful that the devil is crafty. He has details on your life and has seen you respond to certain situations. This isn't to ignite a fear but an awareness. How should this motivate you to respond?

Every time you hear a lie, there is always a question tied to it: *"Will you receive me?"* A repeated attack can be a little more disconcerting and may hit you in a different season in life, colored a little differently. It may even have been rendered dead. How do you address this?

For further study: II Cor. 10:3-5,
Eph. 6:12, Jn. 17:16, Mk. 16:17:18.

*As you go about your day, ask the Lord
to show you how much he loves you.*

DAY 24

The Flesh Profits Nothing

Jesus said to him, "I am the way, and the truth, and the life…"

John 14:6a ESV

When I read this verse, I can almost hear Jesus say, *"Carrie, I love you so much that I made it easy for you; I am the only way. Your search for answers, for help, and whatever else you need starts and stops with Me."* God made it easy for all of us.

Every day brings an opportunity to *not* choose His way. Doing so is foolishness, but we tend to do it anyway. It's not necessarily because we wake up and declare that we will not choose His way; we all have this fleshly body and fallen world to live in. We can list pages of what can trigger a demand on the flesh.

The "ugly" side of the word *flesh* quickly brings to mind every facet of sin. But I want to address two dynamics of fleshly responses that sometimes go unchecked.

One response is when we find ourselves as everyone's problem solver. I am the oldest of six children and I helped raise my siblings; so, I understand this well. I would mastermind how to do things better and created working solutions that benefitted everyone.

However, this developed into perfectionism. I was constantly putting a demand on myself to do things perfectly at home, at church, or before people. There was an unspoken pressure to do things right; and when things were done correctly, people became dependent.

It wasn't until my late teens or early college years that I got a revelation: *I am not the way, the truth, or the life.* God is. I am not supposed to fix everything.

When people become dependent on us, we become their solution and hinder them from seeking out their true Source.

> "My grace is for you, but not on what you are presently putting your hands on and being in full control of it." God cannot bless pride.

Burn-out, frustration, and self-reliance follow because an *only-I-can-do-this* mindset sets in. We grow anxious of people's expectations or see that things need to be done our way. No tools have been provided for them to manage without us because there hasn't been time. We've just been too busy doing everything *for* them!

The other area the flesh rises is when we get busy doing our agenda and ask God to bless everything our hands touch. Or He has told something specific and we attempt to do it in our own wisdom and timing. In either instance, we have taken control and followed our version of truth.

Holding onto control might seem like a convenient way for things to move along without delays. Things seem favorable because things are turning out according to our plans; but the devil's fingerprint are all over it. He will let us taste success only to drop a bomb later.

In His love for us, God says, *"My grace is for you, but not on what you are presently putting your hands on and being in full control of it."* God cannot bless pride.

We won't experience the calmness and peace that God has for us when our flesh gets in the way. He is *Truth* so anything that we receive from Him can only be fruitful. But we must follow through on how to carry it out by the leading of the Holy Spirit: *It is the Spirit who gives life; the flesh profits nothing. The words that I speak to you are spirit, and they are life* (John 6:63 NKJV).

Lord, when You say that Your words are spirit and life, this is my call to heed. This is my part in this fight to maintain peace. I am surrendering. I want to keep my relationship with You alive by not missing any opportunity to be in Your presence. Doing this will allow me to get Your very best direction and help keep my flesh from rising.

Are there tendencies you can identify that address some of the fleshly responses we can fall into? What things you are willing to lay down before the Lord?

_____

_____

_____

_____

We may know someone who has allowed their flesh to get in the way of God's best for their lives. If directed by the Holy Spirit, how can you convey His heart on the matter?

For further study:
Col. 2:8.

As you go about your day, remember to ask the Lord to show you how much He loves you.

The Word Births Amazing Faith

So then faith comes by hearing, and hearing by the word of God.

Romans 10:17 NKJV

I really like how this verse puts the word *hearing* twice in the same sentence. Repetition serves as a reminder that being in the Word is a more than a one-time occurrence. The Passion Translation reads: *Faith, then, is birthed in a heart that responds to God's anointed utterance of the Anointed One.*

That is both beautiful and powerful.

Our whole Christian experience is based on responding to God: in intimacy, in scripture meditation, in praise and thanksgiving, in fellowship with other believers. All these serve as a means to encourage, strengthen, and edify. And all of these can contribute to our peace.

> **We have the Head of every kingdom and authority in the universe inside of us!**

But the main contributor to peace is through an ever-increasing faith. Faith comes by hearing (and hearing!) the Word; and the Word gets deeply rooted, fortifying faith. When faith is fortified, it brings peace. This union of faith and peace is forged into a powerful weapon.

I know this firsthand. As soon as I finished Bible College I was gearing up to head to Russia. Here I was, very young, going alone, and with six hundred dollars to my name. I didn't know the language or the culture. I should have been nervous beyond measure.

What others thought about my decision also should have unnerved me. Some people thought I should be married before I left, they questioned how was a young girl going to make it without the skillset of a well-seasoned and well-traveled minister.

I wasn't entirely alone. Another team of graduates went with me, they helped me with my first apartment and things of that nature. I suppose without family present, the door could have swung wide open to loneliness; but honestly, it didn't.

My heart was full of the knowledge of who lived inside of me; I knew that I would never spend one day alone. That comfort and peace bubbled over because *I knew that I knew that I knew.* All of my years growing up and filling my heart with His Word gave me this assurance. I left the States with the notion that I was on an adventure: just me and God!

Knowing that the fullness of the Godhead bodily resides in us as believers is empowering. We have the Head of every kingdom and authority in the universe inside of us! This is foundationally vital to our Christian walk.

We should never view faith as standing and confessing scriptures that, if repeated enough, (and told to the devil enough), belief eventually comes. Yes, faith does come by hearing, but when we are fully established and settled that we have Him with us, we are bold.

Friends and family and our church circles are great, but our faith does not come from their prayers. Faith doesn't come from any faith teacher. Faith comes from the Word. We can surely glean from teachers but we should always be committed to the Word.

As confidence is stirred, we let a transforming work take place, renewing our minds so that our minds and mouths match with the Person living inside. Then we are able to insert every corresponding promise into whatever it is that the devil is trying to steal from our lives: peace, joy, health, finances, relationships.

We have made it clear that the devil roams, looking for people he can lie to in order to separate them from the knowledge of God. We cannot let him have an inch.

The Word births an amazing faith—faith that endures. Let that be our truth today!

Lord, thank You for the full assurance of Your indwelling presence in my life. This encourages me to move forward and take Your Word into every situation I face. I want this great faith to be birthed from my heart because I want to welcome peace into my world…always!

Take some time and dwell on what you just read. Are you experiencing any shifts to you thinking?

Describe how faith and peace become a powerful weapon and how you could apply it to a challenge you may be currently facing?

_____

_____

_____

_____

For further study:
Col. 2:8-9, I Pet. 5:8.

Be sure to ask the Lord to show you
just how much He loves you today!

Hide the Word

Truly, I say to you, whoever says to this mountain,
'Be taken up and thrown into the sea,' and does not
doubt in his heart, but believes that what he says
will come to pass, it will be done for him.

Mark 11:23 ESV

J esus spoke this truth to His disciples after Peter noticed the withered fig tree Jesus had previously cursed. The fig tree responded to the authority of Jesus: *May no one ever eat fruit from you again* (verse 14).

If we have lived long enough, we have had the opportunity to place faith in things other than God: our jobs, education, relationships; talents and giftings, our government. The world is changing fast and putting faith in anything else *but* God, is like putting faith in shifting sand (Matthew 7:26-27).

The one we most readily put faith in is ourselves. We know exactly what we have experienced so we speak faith from experience. *I haven't done anything worth noting, I'm a nobody... He'll never change, it's useless... This lifestyle is freeing, I don't have to commit...Let me fix it, I fix everything.*

We cannot depend on the things we have experienced in life, good or bad, to be the basis for our version of truth. Proverbs 3:5-7 are familiar verses where we are told not to lean on our own understanding. I like how The Passion Translation renders it:

Trust in the Lord completely, and do not rely on our own opinions. With all your heart rely on him to guide you, and he will lead you in every decision you make. Become intimate with him in whatever you do, and he will lead you wherever you go. Don't think for a moment that you know it all.

Leaning on our own understanding is falling. The surest way to *not* gravitate to what we *think* we know is to keep God's Word hidden in our hearts.

I think what draws me to these verses in Proverbs is verse 6 where it says to *become intimate* with Him in whatever we do and He will lead us. He will lead us

> Leaning on our own understanding is falling.

back to the promises that we have hidden in our hearts. If we don't have His truth hidden in abundance and to overflowing, we give the Holy Spirit nothing to bring to our remembrance. We will have nothing to withdraw when confusing times hit.

I briefly touched on Matthew 7:26-27 about shifting sand but I believe we should read it in its full context here. Jesus is speaking:

But everyone who hears my teaching and does not apply it to his life can be compared to a foolish man who built his house on sand. When it rained and the flood came, with wind and waves beating upon his house, it collapsed and was swept away.

A foolish man is one who leans on his own understanding. He has heard the Word, has been given many examples, has heard many testimonials, but he still goes back to do life in his own wisdom, his own truth. Leaning on self doesn't produce peace.

The Word of God changes everything, nothing is impossible with God. There is no back up plan. This is how we walk with the peace of God.

What God's grace accomplished made it possible for us to sit in heavenly places. If we can see ourselves seated with Him, we are the ones looking down on problems. We don't tell our mountain how big it is; rather we tell our mountain how big our God is!

This is the conquering perspective God desires for His children. He already accomplished the work! We believe it, apply it, and rest in that truth. Peace is ours!

Lord, I'm choosing to trust what was accomplished for me and will stop focusing on problems, distractions, and the lies I have spoken to myself. My prior experience will not be the basis for truth. Only Your Word. Help me, Holy Spirt to settle this in my heart once and for all.

I believe that you are getting a full dose of truth! Has there been anything new you have learned today that has shown you that God is the God of His Word? Be sure to hide it in your heart.

_____

_____

_____

_____

When the devil sees us, he sees Jesus. But what we say may not sound like Jesus, thereby giving the enemy a foothold. How can that be remedied by what has been discussed today?

For further study:
Ps. 119:11, Mk. 11:12-14, Jn. 17:17.

Ask the Lord to show you how
much He loves you today!

DAY 27

Reflect

Much of what we have been discussing the past couple of days has covered our authority and being purposeful to dismiss our own truth. I believe Albert Einstein is credited for the quote: *Insanity is doing the same thing over and over and expecting different results.*

I feel that this is the hamster wheel many of us find ourselves on. We have heard the truth and have seen it prosper in another person's life. But when it comes to our own lives, we find that we haven't relinquished control.

Our effort profits zero. It gets in the way of cutting off the heads of the giants in our lives. There needs to be a new paradigm that governs how we operate. That paradigm is the Word that has been hidden and meditated on. The Word produces great faith if we let it.

Ponder again on the accomplishment of Christ. Does the spirit of a shepherd boy rise within? Can you say that you know your God, know the strength of your God, and trust in the delivering power of your God? With all that has been discussed in days 22-26, where do you find yourself seated?

All authority was given to Jesus. He gave it to us!

DAY 28

Reveal

God is for us and never leaves us, but He does expect us to use our spiritual authority. Our spiritual authority is revealed in our spoken word. We don't pray for God to take sickness away; we speak it away!

How awesome it would have been to see the withered fig tree that Jesus cursed. We *are* able to see the attacks on our lives wither up and die in the same manner. Peer into the spiritual realm and see headless and withered giants. Where is the sting of their dance and taunts?

Bring that realization to the here and now. The King of kings reigns and is over every authority. He lives inside of us; therefore, authority is our right.

Meditate on the following verses. Hide them in your heart so that you are able to make confident withdrawals for future attacks. The devil is after your peace. Prep your heart and stay alert and know your position of authority and victory!

Matt. 28:18 NLT: *Jesus came and told his disciples, "I have been given all authority in heaven and on earth."*

_____

_____

_____

_____

Matt. 10:8 TPT: *You must continually bring healing to lepers and to those who are sick, and make it your habit to break off the demonic presence from people, and raise the dead back to life. Freely you have received the power of the kingdom, so freely release it to others.*

_____

_____

_____

_____

Mk. 16:18 ESV: "...*they will speak in new tongues; they will pick up serpents with their hands; and if they drink any deadly poison, it will not hurt them; they will lay their hands on the sick, and they will recover.*"

_____

_____

_____

_____

We are a believing generation,
purposed for this time.

Purposefully Created

I know the plans that I have for you, declares the Lord. They are plans for peace and not disaster, plans to give you a future filled with hope.

Jeremiah 29:11 GW

We truly have the victory and can apply peace to every aspect of our lives. When the world is at literal war or warring within their person, we have someone bigger living inside. And He is someone we ought to share with others.

Every gift of God is our inheritance: wisdom, knowledge, courage; healing, prosperity, provision. These gifts contain peace and bring peace with them when we declare them over our situations. We may not see the immediate change to our circumstances, but peace is definitely attached to our words when speaking of what is rightfully ours.

Jeremiah 29:11 is one of those scriptures that has much promise attached to it. It is a scripture we can wield when peace is being attacked. It has been one I have used.

I recall the first time I received a deep revelation of this verse. I was very young when I declared that I was going to be a missionary. No other desire burned so passionately. But around the time of my early teens, the ugly head of comparison popped up and I began to second guess this hold on my heart. The devil was sure to keep my mind distracted with what I was seeing.

But in God's infinite love for my teenaged self, He told me that when He declares something, it is packed with supernatural, creative ability and abundantly supplied with extraordinary miracle might! And not just this verse, but every declared promise and truth He has ever spoken.

This is *not* for the declarations you have in mind for your future: how *your* healing regimen will take place in your body; how *your* plans and infinite wisdom will save your marriage. Only

> We need a working knowledge of the Word because peace will follow the truth we know.

His Word goes out and achieves what it is intended to accomplish.

This verse was one of my biggest weapons that I used repeatedly when my sister was hospitalized with Covid. The devil thought he had me because my heart was cut deeply. I would go to her room to pray and I would see my beautiful sister, on a ventilator, swollen beyond recognition.

My fight was to declare all these promises in the Bible, to declare that our God had these wonderful promises for her; that she was going raise her kids and see the good plans that God had for her children. Her children's future had their mother in it! This was not her destiny, for she was purposely created for more—a future filled with hope!

These words I declared were *His* declarations, they were truth. When we are secure in that, we can drown out the lies of the enemy, turn off the opinions of others, and silence the limits we place on ourselves. We need a working knowledge of the Word because peace will follow the truth we know.

If God be for us, who can be against us? We have His plans for peace and not disaster, for a future filled with immeasurably more. We are purposefully created and have a tomorrow full of potential; but we have today to make His declarations now!

Lord, Your Word is packed with wisdom and creative grace and power. You have declared my future with peace and have purposed only good things in it. Help me not to hinder anything by my words or the words of others. Help me to keep Your Word as my highest value.

The enemy truly wants to keep you limited; he sees and knows your potential! You may have a hard time seeing potential as God's gift; but today that stops. Make some powerful declarations now!

Jeremiah 29:11 is a powerful weapon. Can you identify more weapons in His Word that you can add to your *weapons-of-peace* arsenal?

_____

_____

_____

_____

For further study:
Is. 55:11, II Pet. 3:9, Matt. 5:13-16, Rom. 8:31-39.

As you go about your day, ask the Lord to show you how much He loves you today!

More Than a Conqueror

Yet in all these things we are more than conquerors through Him who loved us. For I am persuaded that neither death nor life, nor angels nor principalities nor powers, nor things present nor things to come, nor height nor depth, nor any other created thing, shall be able to separate us from the love of God which is in Christ Jesus our Lord.

Romans 8:37-39 NKJV

Being persuaded that nothing can ever separate us from the love of God positions us in a totally different level of victory. This brings a rest and peace that develops into an attitude of faith and expectancy.

In II Peter 1:2, Peter addresses his letter to people of like faith. His salutation begins: *May grace and peace be multiplied to you in the knowledge of God and of Jesus our Lord.* His letter then continues to challenge and encourage. Can I encourage you; as you respond to the Holy Spirit's daily invitation to relationship, there is multiplied grace and peace for you. Multiplied!

> Great is our peace!

Greater is He who is in us, the Prince of Peace, and King of the universe. These describe the might of our God—an abundant God—who chose to make His dwelling within us to show Himself in an abundant way. We are not destined for mere slivers of anything.

As we grow in the knowledge of what Jesus died to give us, and how that love was the ultimate purpose behind the cross, we rise! We stand and speak the promises of our inheritance, mediating and confessing them over and over so that they become part of our thought processes. Not just an awareness; but a knowing that becomes a part of our person.

Our resolve and authority become the backbone of our resistance to the lies of the enemy. We don't have to live with fear, defeat, frustration, offense and judgment. When we live and thrive in a relationship where we are constantly being filled with wisdom and understanding, we are enabled to stand and take our positions of peace: *Great is our peace!*

Being fully persuaded is how we fight with peace! There is no shadow of a doubt that God is with us and for us. The devil will still attempt to deceive us; but we will recognize it in a heartbeat. We don't let him tire us out; we stand and keep standing (Ephesians 6:13).

The following is a story illustrating bits and pieces of things that have been shared in this series. We see persistence in contending for a declared victory; we see how letting positive imagination brings forth a future reality. This is a story of God saying to us, *"Let me serve you in this way: be still, and know that I am God."*

The Conqueror

A boxer decided to pursue his dream of becoming the Heavy Weight Champion of the World. His time as an amateur boxer gained him some notoriety. He was a powerhouse in his weight class and won several fights; but he knew he was destined for more. So, he began training.

His training was disciplined and outright rigorous—every fatigued part of his body and every aching muscle screamed at him, *"I hate you!"* But that didn't stop him. Training was carried into real fights at the local level just for experience. His face bore the look of a wearied fighter: missing teeth, broken facial bones, Vaseline smeared over swollen and slit eyelids. To others, scary. To him, just the beginning. He was always hungry for the next bout.

At every fight he looked stronger, leaner, and meaner. Technique and speed had developed. He still got bruised and banged up. *Tired?* Yes, but it never really fazed him. A focused mind had been part of his training. He knew what waited in his future: the title, the belt. That had been his focus. He contended for the dream; he would do whatever it took.

The world grew increasingly amazed at the talent of this once-amateur-now-turned-pro boxer. He won round after round, bloodied match after bloodied match. PR dubbed him as *The Conqueror* because he packed a surprisingly devastating punch. He was marketed as the next "big thing." Every fight that followed, he didn't disappoint. He lived up to the brand.

Finally, the day came to lock horns with the reigning champion. His trainer sized up the opponent—he was a powerhouse in his own right. He took his fighter aside and looked him straight in the eyes, *"Listen, you are The Conqueror. You get in that ring and you take care of this guy. You're going in; you are not falling down. You are not losing. You are coming out of that ring with a belt and you are going to be the Heavy Weight Champion of the World!"*

His trainer's words mixed with his own faith. This was what he trained for, what he sweated for, what he bled for. There was no shadow of a doubt. This was his fight.

Ding! Game on.

Punch. Dodge. Sway. The fighters did their boxing dance and taunted with their gloves. The crowd was loving it. The bout got more aggressive and more exciting. The Conqueror took a severe hit to his right eye, then a powerful lip-splitting jab. His resolve only grew stronger.

Uppercuts; more strikes across his face. A blow to his ribs. All the while he thought: title, belt. But his opponent's hits kept coming. Forcefully;

almost deadly. The Conqueror's mind became a force like never before.

The two battered and bruised fighters came from their corners and entered the sixth round;

The Conqueror was stoic. The crowd had seen that look before; and they leaned forward wide-eyed and waited with bated breath.

The Conqueror delivered his opponent *the* conquering blow. His opponent's head turned sharply to the right; his mouth guard flew out as if yanked with an invisible string. A slobbering, red mess soared through the air, causing ringside cameras to wildly click in rapid succession. His opponent hit the canvas.

The referee completed his count. The fight was over and The Conqueror's arm was raised in victory. The crowd went crazy. The media was up in a whirlwind: "*What's it like being the Heavy Weight Champion?*" "*People are saying rematch… what do you say?*" "*Who will you fight next?*"

After all the hoopla and a soothing shower, the champ got ready to go home. His trainer entered the locker room with the commissioner of the event, "*You did it! You're The Conqueror; you made it!"* The commissioner handed the fighter two envelopes. The champ opened the first one. Nice check. The second one contained a wad of cash. The champ smiled in gratitude. The trainer grabbed the belt and threw it over The Conqueror's shoulder, *"You've earned it!"*

The champ got in his car; sore but satisfied. He listened to the news on the radio and it was all about him and how he conquered. He smiled and thought: *Yeah, I did this.*

At home, he was greeted at the door by his loving wife. She grimaced at his face, but smiled. She knew. *"Baby,"* he said, *"I have conquered them all to get to this place!"* She continued to smile and held out her hand. He pulled out the check and the cash. He placed them in her hand.

Do you know what she is at that moment? She is more than a conqueror. She didn't have to fight for the reward. She didn't have suffer the bloody and excruciating beating for it. No wounds, no scars. That is what these verses in Romans chapter eight are talking about.

Jesus accomplished everything for us. Jesus took the scourging and was martyred for us so that we could be more than conquerors. He bore all suffering so that we could stand in His promises. The promises from the cross are yes, and amen. We are conquerors over every situation today, no matter what comes against us. What He did for us was an accomplishing work—done once and for all. We can rest in that accomplishment because Jesus has declared our peace by the blood of the cross!

Lord God, I am more than a conqueror! That is my declaration. There are truly no words to convey my heart when I consider Your sacrifice! Even if I were to have been the only one, You still would have endured it all. Be still, and know that I am God… these words have taken on a different meaning for me today. As I rest in Your accomplished work, I am stilled, and I understand that You will always be my God in every season, in every circumstance, no matter what. I am forever blessed!

You are more than a conqueror! How will you carry yourself knowing that as Jesus hung on the cross, His mind was on you? What does your heart want to tell Him?

_____

_____

_____

_____

Be still, and know that I am God (Psalm 46:10a). How does this verse minister to your heart?

_____

_____

_____

_____

For further study:

Go back and review all the scriptures in this series. Hide the Word in your heart and remind the Holy Spirit to help you recall all that you have learned.

Don't ever let a day go by without asking the Lord to show you how much he loves you!

Receive Jesus as Your Savior

Choosing to receive Jesus Christ as your Lord and Savior is the most important decision you'll ever make!

God's Word promises, *"That if thou shalt confess with thy mouth the Lord Jesus, and shalt believe in thine heart that God hath raised him from the dead, thou shalt be saved. For with the heart man believeth unto righteousness; and with the mouth confession is made unto salvation" (Rom. 10:9–10). "For whosoever shall call upon the name of the Lord shall be saved"* (Rom. 10:13). By His grace, God has already done everything to provide salvation. Your part is simply to believe and receive.

Pray out loud: "Jesus, I confess that You are my Lord and Savior. I believe in my heart that God raised You from the dead. By faith in Your Word, I receive salvation now. Thank You for saving me."

The very moment you commit your life to Jesus Christ, the truth of His Word instantly comes to pass in your spirit. Now that you're born again, there's a brand-new you!

Receive
the Holy Spirit

As His child, your loving heavenly Father wants to give you the supernatural power you need to live a new life. *"For every one that asketh receiveth; and he that seeketh findeth; and to him that knocketh it shall be opened…how much more shall your heavenly Father give the Holy Spirit to them that ask him?"* (Luke 11:10–13).

All you have to do is ask, believe, and receive!

Pray this: "Father, I recognize my need for Your power to live a new life. Please fill me with Your Holy Spirit. By faith, I receive it right now. Thank You for baptizing me. Holy Spirit, You are welcome in my life."

Congratulations! Now you're filled with God's supernatural power.

Some syllables from a language you don't recognize will rise up from your heart to your mouth (1 Cor. 14:14). As you speak them out loud by faith, you're releasing God's power from within and building yourself up in the spirit (1 Cor. 14:4). You can do this whenever and wherever you like.

It doesn't really matter whether you felt anything or not when you prayed to receive the Lord and His Spirit. If you believed in your heart that you received, then God's Word promises you did. *"Therefore I say unto you, What things soever ye desire, when ye pray, believe that ye receive them, and ye shall have them"* (Mark 11:24). God always honors His Word—believe it!

Please contact me and let me know that you've prayed to receive Jesus as your Savior or be filled with the Holy Spirit. I would like to rejoice with you and help you understand more fully what has taken place in your life. I'll send you a free gift that will help you understand and grow in your new relationship with the Lord.

Welcome to your new life!

Call for Prayer

If you need prayer for any reason, you can call our Prayer Line 24 hours a day, seven days a week at 719-635-1111. A trained prayer minister will answer your call and pray with you. Every day, we receive testimonies of healings and other miracles from our Prayer Line, and we are ministering God's nearly-too-good-to-be-true message of the Gospel to more people than ever. So I encourage you to call today!

How does one receive a revelation of God's love? Is it only for those who are destined for a great purpose? Is it simply emotions or memorization? Or for those who qualify?

In this Scriptural Devotional the Word simply speaks God's heart and love to you. That you are loved because "He is love" (1 John 4:8). That you were so loved that He gave His son for you (John 3:16). That His perfect love casts out all fear (1 John 4:18) and His abundant love has been poured out within your hearts by the Holy Spirit (Romans 5:5).

These verses are straight from God's heart to you—His love letter. If you allow your mind and heart to be transformed by these verses, you will forever walk with the revelation attitude and confidence that you are loved by God!

Also from
CARRIE PICKETT

Lifestyle of Intimacy is a daily devotional that will help you discover how much God desires to show what salvation really provided... relationship. Relationship with God... what a concept!

You can know the heart, will, and voice of not only The Living, All-Powerful God, but your God, your Savior, your Father! What a beautiful invitation from your Redeemer. In this devotional learn how to respond daily to His love and walk in greater relationship and everyday victory.

life FOUNDATIONS
with Carrie Pickett

Join Carrie as she uncovers the foundational principles of the Word of God and discover how these truths can transform your everyday life.

Scan the QR code to watch full episodes of Life Foundations

CONTACT INFORMATION

Charis Bible College

800 Gospel Truth Way

Woodland Park, CO 80863

info@charisbiblecollege.org

Helpline Available 24/7: 719-635-1111

CharisBibleCollege.org

Also visit Carrie at CarriePickett.com